A RESOURCE FROM

The Southern Baptist Theological Seminary

MORE
FAITHFUL
SERVICE

THIS WORKBOOK BELONGS TO:

_____

IF FOUND, PLEASE CONTACT:

_____

EMAIL   PHONE NUMBER

SBTS PRESS

THIS IS A DIFFERENT SORT OF BOOK.

Or workbook. Or journal. Whatever it is, it's meant to help you grow in more faithful gospel ministry. And it's meant for you to use and devour. You'll notice pages with blank space; those pages are for you to respond to questions, react to the quotations, and reflect on the Scripture references you'll find throughout.

So, open your Bible, get out your pen, and fan into flame your desire to fulfill this most noble and weighty task.

FAITHF

PART ONE

ULNESS

Only one life, 'twill
soon be past /
Only what's done for
Christ will last.

C.T. STUDD

WHAT IS THE ROAD TO FAITHFULNESS?

BY

R. ALBERT MOHLER JR.

THE STUDY

We must rehear the Bible and reimagine the concept of successful ministry not as necessarily immediately fruitful but as demonstrably faithful to God's Word.

MARK DEVER

A preacher who pursues a course of solid thinking, who nourishes his mind by various reading, will always be interesting.

ALEXANDRE RODOLPHE VINET

The pastor must study, study, study, or he will not grow, or even live, as a true workman for Christ.

THOMAS MURPHY

Those whom God calls into ministry are not called to manufacture results, to design program after program, or to work their way into bigger churches. The primary aim of any minister of the gospel is faithfulness: to the gospel, to the people in his care, to his family, and to his Savior. And yet the temptation exists to be something less than faithful. The lure of shortcuts and small concessions can be strong, but these moves of seeming insignificance lead only to serious compromise and disaster. A pressing question faces every gospel minister:

WILL YOU PURSUE FAITHFULNESS, OR WILL YOU GIVE WAY TO COMPROMISE?

The life of faithful service is a life of study, and it has been so from the very beginning. The Apostle Paul instructed Timothy to study so that he could present himself to God as an approved worker, "a worker who has no need to be ashamed" (2 Tim 2:15). This instruction came within the context of Timothy's call as a preacher and teacher of God's Word, and Paul's instruction to Timothy is our Lord's instruction to all who would serve God's people.

A word of honesty is necessary at this point. Any honest assessment of the contemporary church would indicate that vast numbers of ministers serving Christ's church are derelict in this duty. They are intellectually lazy, biblically illiterate, slothful in their study habits, and they often steal the learning of others in order to hide their own disobedience. This is a scandal that robs the congregation of the learned and faithful ministry the people of God so desperately need and deserve.

The pastor's lifetime of study begins with the moment of his call and properly ends only when he breathes his last breath. Between the call and the grave lies a long and rewarding journey of faithful learning – learning that will be put at the disposal of the congregation until we see our Lord face to face.

> The duties of this office are such that it is impossible to discharge them effectively without a life of close study. ... Nothing will take the place of laborious and persevering study for the faithful discharge of the duties of this office.
>
> THOMAS MURPHY

Do you have time worked into your day to read and study? In what ways do you intentionally grow in loving and serving God with your mind?

> Our aim in studying the Godhead must be to know God himself better. Our concern must be to enlarge our acquaintance, not simply with the doctrine of God's attributes, but with the living God whose attributes they are.
>
> J.I. PACKER

> I count everything as loss because of the surpassing worth of knowing Christ Jesus my Lord.
>
> PHILIPPIANS 3:8

KNOWING GOD

> Be sure to feed your own soul. Don't think first about how the Word feeds others but let God restore and strengthen you through his Word. If we neglect time in the Word and prayer, then we will wither and grow cold and brittle in our relationship with God.
>
> THOMAS R. SCHREINER

The preacher's first task is to know God personally. The Bible has no conception of an unconverted ministry. The preacher is first of all a man who has come to know God through faith in the Lord Jesus Christ, and who finds his greatest fulfillment in knowing God personally and redemptively.

God told the prophet Jeremiah, "Let him who boasts boast in this, that he understands and knows me" (Jer 9:24). Our fundamental knowledge is a knowledge of God, and this is the central goal of all true theological education and ministry preparation. The minister must be one who sets his sight on a vibrant personal knowledge of God. Otherwise, theological knowledge becomes a ground for personal pride and intellectual pretentiousness.

This approach to the minister's life of study brings a godly sense of balance. Our central aim is to know God, and the aim of our ministry is to lead our people to know God also. The other aspects of knowledge are useful only in so far as they lead us into a deeper knowledge of God. A healthy theological education inculcates a deeper love for God, even as the minister grows in the knowledge of God's Word and the comprehensiveness of God's truth.

What are your personal devotional habits? Do you make time to read the Word for the sake of your own soul and not just for preparation? How does a neglect of these duties affect your spiritual health?

> Whether you like it or not, read and pray daily. It is for your life; there is no other way, else you will be a trifler all your days and a petty, superficial preacher. Do justice to your own soul; give it time and means to grow; do not starve yourself any longer.
>
> JOHN WESLEY

> All Scripture is breathed out by God and profitable for teaching, for reproof, for correction, and for training in righteousness, that the man of God may be complete, equipped for every good work.
>
> 2 TIMOTHY 3:16-17

> Incline my heart to your testimonies, and not to selfish gain! Turn my eyes from looking at worthless things; and give me life in your ways.
>
> PSALM 119:36-37

STUDYING GOD'S WORD

> Study the Bible, dear brethren, through and through, with all the helps that you can possibly obtain: remember that the appliances now within the reach of ordinary Christians are much more extensive than they were in our fathers' days, and therefore you must be greater biblical scholars if you would keep in front of your hearers. Intermeddle with all knowledge, but above all things meditate day and night in the law of the Lord.
>
> CHARLES H. SPURGEON

Paul's instruction to Timothy was very clear. The young minister was to study in order that he would be found "rightly handling the Word of truth" (2 Tim 2:15). A deep and growing knowledge of God's Word is the indispensable ground of all other true knowledge.

Put simply, the pastor is to be a devoted and skillful student of the Scripture. This is the most important field of knowledge for the pastor, for his primary task is to preach the Word "in season and out of season" (2 Tim 4:2) and to teach God's people from God's Word.

Clearly, this strategic call represents a stewardship of truth, souls, and calling. Failure in this task is beyond tragedy, and the consequences are eternal. There are ancient paths of truth on which the pastor must walk, and the call of faithfulness is the call to stick to those ancient paths and lead our people on them.

This is a demanding calling, and nothing less than the most serious life of study will do. The subject of the pastor's study is the inspired Word of God.

The preacher must be more knowledgeable and more skilled than his congregation. While there are many fields of knowledge and intellectual stimulation to which we could give our attention, we must keep ourselves first and foremost students of the Bible.

What are ways you can grow in your knowledge of the Bible and of orthodoxy? Are there books you should read, courses you should take, and passages you should memorize?

List a few action steps below for ways to deepen your knowledge of God's Word.

I will most gladly spend
and be spent for your souls.

2 CORINTHIANS 12:15 "

SERVING GOD'S PEOPLE

Christ loved the souls of
men, and had so great a
regard to their salvation, that
he thought it worthy for him
so to lay out himself. Shall not
his ministers and servants be
willing to do the same?

JONATHAN EDWARDS

"

Ultimately, the pastor's calling is a call to serve the people of God in faithfulness. And that call requires the pastor to commit himself and his ministry to the Scripture and to the faith delivered to the saints. The pastor who gives his mind and heart to the Bible will serve with greater effectiveness and greater faithfulness.

This is no easy task. That's surely why Paul used the metaphors of the soldier, the athlete, and the farmer as he described this calling to Timothy (2 Tim 2:3-7). We are called to the obedience of the soldier, the discipline of the athlete, and the patient endurance of the farmer.

We should note carefully that Paul describes the ministry this way just before commanding Timothy to study in order to show himself faithful. May we, like Timothy, do our best to present ourselves to God as workers who have no need to be ashamed.

How have you seen "small" compromises make an impact in your ministry? How can you avoid and change the patterns in your life that lead to compromise?

What would increased faithfulness in your life and ministry look like?

DEAR TIMOTHY

JEFF ROBINSON

Grace to you and peace from God our Father and the Lord Jesus Christ. The last time I wrote you, recall that I sought to stir up your mind by way of reminder, to use the words of our dear brother Peter, that you must find your contentment in Christ alone, else you will be habitually frustrated in your ministry. Remember, that was my first watchword for you in the ministry: contentment. Today, I write to you and commend to you a second, equally vital, watchword: faithfulness.

My dear brother in Christ, the world will try to press you into its God-denying mold when it comes to gauging your success in ministry. The world, and perhaps a good many well-meaning but carnal-minded people in your congregation, will tell you that for your ministry to be con-

sidered a success, you will have to exhibit regular conversions to Christ, have a lakeshore lined with candidates for baptism, and possess attendance numbers that increase astronomically overnight within your congregation. They will seek to sell you on the notion that those are the marks of ministerial success, and you may be allured by such cheap reasoning. Don't buy it.

While we certainly desire healthy church rolls and want to see untold numbers experience the effectual grace of Christ, you must remember that conversion and church growth are God's business. (Recall what happened after Pentecost when God added more than 3,000 to his church in one day? Wasn't that glorious?) Those may be measures of what God is doing in your ministry, but not necessarily. Recall the false prophets I have warned you about, the ones who have roiled the church in Ephesus, and remember also those super apostles with whom I contended at the church in Corinth? They were gaining quite a following, and who among us would assume that the fruit of their false teaching was healthy?

Timothy, God is not calling you to be omnipotent, for you are merely a weak clay pot; common, expendable crockery. God is not calling you to be omniscient, for all men are ignorant to such a degree that James had to remind us that he who makes plans without considering God's sovereignty is sinfully presumptuous. God is not calling you to be omnipresent, for you minister in vain if you seek to be everywhere all at once out of a sinful fear of man. God is not calling you to please men, for men are fickle. The church members who are today praising you are just as likely to be calling for your ouster when your ministry threatens to upset the peace within the kingdoms over which they occupy the throne. He is not calling you to earn their praise. You must please him alone. God is not calling you to fear men. You must fear him. If you will fear God and nothing else and hate sin and nothing else, God may turn the world upside down through your ministry.

No, God is calling you simply to be faithful. He is calling you to be faithful in feeding and leading his flock. Remember, it is his flock. It is his kingdom, not yours. You have been called to build it, by his grace, faithfully. What does such faithfulness entail? It's not going to look like that which the world calls "success," and you must settle this notion in your heart and mind now. God has called you to faithfulness in preaching his Word, being ready at all times to proclaim his truth. Forsaking all else, God has called you to set the oracles of God before the people of God to the glory of God every Lord's Day. Do not worry about results. Results are God's business. He has called you to faithfulness in studying to show yourself approved, a workman who is able to rightly divide his Word. That will always be priority one: Many hours in study and prayer will

> God is not calling you to fear men. You must fear him. If you will fear God and nothing else and hate sin and nothing else, God may turn the world upside down through your ministry.
>
> **JEFF ROBINSON**

establish you in this crucial endeavor. He has called you to be faithful in guarding the gospel he has deposited into your care, which means you must know sound doctrine and teach sound doctrine. He has called you to be faithful in refuting false doctrine as well. Therefore, my dear son, you must work hard to be a pastor-theologian. That is an irreducible part of faithfulness in ministry. Studying God's Word and learning theology are hard work, but such labors will pay dividends into eternity, for this is the way God, in his infinite wisdom, has ordained it.

So God is calling you to be faithful in guarding your doctrine, but he is also calling you to be faithful in keeping a close watch over your life and conduct, what Solomon in Proverbs calls "guarding your heart with all vigilance." Though you are young, you must be faithful in living out the theology of grace that has been given to you through God's Word. Will your people find your theology compelling if the theology you claim to hold dear has had little discernible effect on your life? How can you commend grace to others if you are not willing to live a godly, gracious lifestyle? A man of grace must be a gracious man, a wise and godly sage once told me.

You must be faithful in asking God to form those character traits in you that I passed down to you in another letter, traits that God gave me as qualifications for his undershepherds. You must be a faithful family man; loving your wife as Christ loved the church and training your future children up in the discipline and instruction of the Lord. You must petition our Lord for daily grace in being sober-minded, self-controlled, respectable, hospitable, and gentle. You must plug the ears and shield the eyes of your heart to the deadly lure of money, and you must be able to teach and debate the truth with others in a gracious and winsome matter. Living out these attributes by God's grace and praying that God will bear the full range of the fruit of his Spirit in you are all part of what it means to be a faithful herald of God's Word.

And you must persevere in faithfulness even when war has broken out all around you in the ministry. Remember, you are a soldier of Christ. Until our Lord returns, you will be at war, not at peace. Thus, you must fight the good fight of faith on behalf of yourself and your people. You must persevere in loving the members of your congregation, even those irascible, incorrigible souls who withhold love from you and defame your good name to others. Remember what I told the church at Corinth: Love bears all things, believes all things, hopes all things, endures all things. You must love them with the kind of selfless love that compelled our Savior to the cross.

Timothy, no matter what the world tells you, no matter what well-meaning church people tell you, if you do all these things consistently, you will then be a worker approved by God who need not be ashamed, no matter the size of your church or the scope of your ministry. You will adorn the gospel, your message, with the sweet aroma of Christ. I close with the same words of encouragement that I told to the Corinthians, for it is a helpful summary of the Christian man's call to faithfulness: Be watchful, stand firm in the faith, act like a man, be strong. Let all that you do be done in love.

There is much more I could say, but I pray this pithy encouragement will steel your frame toward the pursuit of faithfulness. May God make you content in his Son and faithful to the end in proclaiming his Word and shepherding his flock for his glory. May our invincible sovereign Lord make his face to shine on you and your labors. Grace be with you.

Faithfully your father in the faith,

PAUL

YOU WILL THEN BE A WORKER APPROVED BY GOD WHO NEED NOT BE ASHAMED, NO MATTER THE SIZE OF YOUR CHURCH OR THE SCOPE OF YOUR MINISTRY. YOU WILL ADORN THE GOSPEL, YOUR MESSAGE, WITH THE SWEET AROMA OF CHRIST.

But I do not account my life of any value nor as precious to myself, if only I may finish my course and the ministry that I received from the Lord Jesus, to testify to the gospel of the grace of God.

ACTS 20:24

Though the words of the wise be as nails fastened by the masters of assemblies, yet their examples are the hammer to drive the nails in to take a deeper hold.

THOMAS FULLER

PERSIS

PART TWO

TENCE

> Success in spiritual work is not synonymous with being in the public eye or even being regarded by God's people as successful. Success is finishing the work God has given us, and no one else, to do.

DEREK PRIME AND ALISTAIR BEGG "

10 MARKS OF PERSISTENT PASTORAL LEADERSHIP

BY

HERSHAEL W. YORK

PEOPLE TRUST
LEADERS THEY
BELIEVE WILL
BE THERE IN
THE FUTURE.

Ministry burnout is a sad reality. There are a host of external issues that often combine to make a ministry post impossible to endure, but often those issues are a result of the minister's own failures.

The strongest churches in America are those who have enjoyed continuous, persistent, and strong pastoral leadership. Regardless of denomination or leadership model, the most obvious common denominator is that leaders persisted and stayed long enough to harvest the vision they planted. People trust leaders they believe will be there in the future.

When Paul described the burden of ministry that God has given us, he concluded by asking the question, "Who is equal to such a task?" (2 Cor 2:16) After reviewing the challenges of leadership in the church, we might ask the same thing. We must remember, however, that wherever God calls, he also enables. God did not call us to be fruitless and unprofitable. He has a plan and purpose for his leaders, and leadership can be more effective if we follow some very practical and thoroughly scriptural guidelines. These guidelines could be a means of God giving you the grace you need to persist where you are.

KNOW WHERE YOU ARE GOING.

Uncertainty is not an unusual circumstance. That doesn't mean, though, that in those moments the pastor's ministry grinds to a halt. To the contrary, the pastor will find the routine matters of ministry are more important than ever. A pastor will find it far better to do the obvious things that one knows God wants — preach the Word, visit the sick, witness to the lost, build relationships — than to proceed with a plan that he is not confidently convinced is of the Lord.

Don't have a building program just because others are doing it. Don't follow the latest trend because you read it in a book and it seems to be working for another church. If you lead the church down too many blind paths, the price you pay will be ineffectiveness and irrelevant leadership. Be certain that you know where God wants the church to go.

How are you doing in the "obvious things" that God calls you to do? Do you have a clear sense of where your church is going, or are you inclined to make decisions impulsively?

> Keep a close watch on yourself and on the teaching. Persist in this, for by so doing you will save both yourself and your hearers.
>
> 1 TIMOTHY 4:16

WHATEVER A CHURCH LEADER DOES, HE MUST NEVER COMPROMISE THE SCRIPTURE FOR HIS OWN PURPOSES.

> Faithfulness demands that we should not become mere pipers to our hearers, playing such tunes as they may demand of us, but should remain as the Lord's mouth to declare all his counsels.
>
> CHARLES SPURGEON

2

BE HONEST WITH THE SCRIPTURE.

Too many pastors have twisted Scripture and assigned meaning foreign to the text and to the author just to get their people to conform. One church was experiencing a steady hemorrhage of members who were leaving and joining another congregation that was larger and seemed to be on the move. The pastor of the smaller church did everything he could to stop the bleeding, but when he sensed that he was unsuccessful, he finally played his trump card — he made it a scriptural issue. His text, however, had nothing to do with churches or membership. He preached about Jesus walking on the water and Peter getting out of the boat, only to sink in failure. The pastor then proceeded to compare the boat to the church, and he said that Peter would not have sunk had he remained in the boat. The lesson was not left for inference. "You better stay in this boat," he told them.

Whatever a church leader does, he must never compromise the Scripture for his own purposes, no matter how noble they may seem at the time. And if he does yield to that temptation and contort a text to lend a false sense of biblical authority to his bad decisions, it will surely come back to haunt him. If a pastor can twist the text, so can the deacons and the church members, often to justify ousting him.

What role does the Scripture play in your ministry (preaching, teaching, counseling, leadership, music)? Does anything need to change to allow the Bible to determine the content of your ministry?

How could your church increase its Word-centeredness?

LIVE A GODLY, HOLY LIFE BEFORE THE PEOPLE.

Godly living is simply right, but it also has the practical value of earning the trust and confidence of the congregation. Once when I was a pastor, I had to make a very difficult decision that I knew would be misunderstood and questioned. Some weeks later a couple in the church came to me and told me that they weren't sure they could stay in the church because they disagreed with the decision I had made. I asked them a pointed question: "Do you believe that I was at least trying to do the right thing and to honor the Lord?" Without hesitation they responded, "Of course. We never doubted that you were doing what you believed to be right. We just think you missed it." I confessed to them that since the matter was not clearly spelled out in Scripture they just might be right. I might get to heaven and discover that I missed it. But at the very least, God would not rebuke me for not seeking and desiring to do his will. "If you trust my heart," I told them, "then you are free to question my decisions, and we still have no problem. As long as you feel that I am seeking God, we can work together, even when we disagree."

Has your conduct earned or undermined the trust of your people? What are some of your areas of weakness that people might observe? Who are some people you could ask to help you evaluate clearly some areas of public weakness?

The whole of our ministry must be carried on in tender love to our people. We must let them see that nothing pleaseth us but what profiteth them.

RICHARD BAXTER

DON'T BE THREATENED BY DISAGREEMENT.

When the Israelites grumbled against Moses and Aaron because they had no food and water, Moses did not get mad at the people. Rather, he marveled they should grumble at him. In the mind of Moses, blame and credit were equally misplaced because he was merely God's servant and instrument. "Who are we," he asked, "that you should grumble against us?" (Ex 16:7). Too often, church leaders are incensed that they should be disputed. Instead of emulating Moses, they ask, "Who are you to question us?" Realize disagreement is healthy, inevitable, and one of the ways God conforms us in his will and to his likeness.

KEEP NEGATIVE EMOTIONS IN CHECK.

Leaders can feel any way they want, but they cannot afford to show the feelings of fear and anger. If a congregation smells fear or anger on the leaders, they will respond in the same way. If attacked in a business meeting, a leader needs to learn the meekness of Moses and the confidence of Nehemiah. In fact, leaders should study biblical leaders like Nehemiah, Moses, David, and Paul to see how they responded in times of adversity and still managed to accomplish the objectives God had given them.

A soft answer turns away wrath,
but a harsh word stirs up anger.

2 CORINTHIANS 12:15

DISAGREEMENT IS HEALTHY, INEVITABLE, AND ONE OF THE WAYS GOD CONFORMS US IN HIS WILL AND TO HIS LIKENESS.

Listen to advice and
accept instruction,
that you may gain
wisdom in the future.

PROVERBS 19:20

What is your instinctive response to disagreement? Do you respond with humility and the ability to learn from the situation? Are you inclined to wear your emotions on your sleeve?

A fool gives full vent to his spirit, but a wise man quietly holds it back.

PROVERBS 29:11

CHOOSE YOUR BATTLES CAREFULLY.

Some battles need to be deferred to a better time, and some need to be ignored completely. Pastors who move on to a church field and immediately make it their goal to "straighten out" every problem they notice either lose their members or lose their job. Never let the direction of your leadership be motivated by your own annoyances. Prioritize and be selective, especially in timing, in what you notice and attempt to change.

BE WILLING TO APOLOGIZE.

There is something very powerful about a leader who is willing to humble himself before his people and say, "I was wrong. Please forgive me." They already know it, but they feel encouraged to see that the leader knows it and does not live under the delusion that he is infallible.

FOCUS ON THE WORD AND THE LOST.

Churches that are well fed are usually more content, and churches that are evangelistic have no time to major on minor issues. Keep the Word and the world on their hearts, and they will be much more easily led. As Max Lucado said, "When fisherman fish, they flourish, and when they don't, they fight."

How have you handled situations and structures in your church that should be changed? Are you hasty to make changes? What battles should you prioritize? Which ones can wait?

> A key to a soldier's survival on the battlefield is to know there are land mines out there and to do whatever he must to avoid stepping on them. The work of ministry is similar in that you can survive a long time if you can avoid stepping on those giant land mines.
>
> BRIAN CROFT

Is there anyone to whom you need to apologize? How have you conveyed to your people that you believe yourself to be infallible?

There are no virtues
wherein your example will
do more than humility and
meekness and self-denial.

RICHARD BAXTER

In what ways is your church focused on the Word and the world?

So I exhort the elders among you, as a fellow elder and a witness of the sufferings of Christ, as well as a partaker in the glory that is going to be revealed: shepherd the flock of God that is among you, exercising oversight, not under compulsion, but willingly, as God would have you; not for shameful gain, but eagerly; not domineering over those in your charge, but being examples to the flock.

1 PETER 1:1-3

What things might be distracting your church from these important things? How can your church grow in prioritizing the Word?

> Just like children require years of slow, patient, repeated teaching in order to grow, so too, normally, does a congregation.
>
> MARK DEVER

DEVELOP LAY LEADERSHIP.

Use the natural units in your church (Sunday School, life groups, deacons, students, women's ministry, etc.) as training grounds for leadership development. Organize five levels of activities that will 1) build relationships, 2) present the gospel, 3) study the Bible, 4) develop leaders, and 5) practice leadership. Just as Moses discovered that he could not do it alone, church leaders must constantly broaden their base of development and ministry sharing.

STAY PUT.

I've said it before, but this is perhaps the single greatest factor in pastoral leadership. The average tenure of a Southern Baptist pastorate is less than four years. Then the church spends six months to a year searching for a pastor. The people develop a resistance to leadership because they see no continuity and feel like they have heard it all before — and often they have because a new pastor has no regard or even knowledge of what his predecessors taught.

> Convinced of this, I know that I will remain and continue with you all, for your progress and joy in the faith, so that in me you may have ample cause to glory in Christ Jesus, because of my coming to you again.

PHILIPPIANS 1:25-26

Are there leaders in whom you invest time and energy? Are you slow to delegate and give opportunities for others to lead?

I have fought the good fight, I have finished the race, I have kept the faith. Henceforth there is laid up for me the crown of righteousness, which the Lord, the righteous judge, will award to me on that Day, and not only to me but also to all who have loved his appearing.

2 TIMOTHY 4:7-8

Who are some of the most important lay leaders in your church? Who are some others the Lord might be raising up to lead?

He gave the apostles, the prophets, the evangelists, the shepherds and teachers, to equip the saints for the work of ministry, for building up the body of Christ.

EPHESIANS 4:11-12

JUST AS MOSES DISCOVERED THAT HE COULD NOT DO IT ALONE, CHURCH LEADERS MUST CONSTANTLY BROADEN THEIR BASE OF DEVELOPMENT AND MINISTRY SHARING.

O Brethren! Who would not study and pray, spend and be spent, in the service of such a bountiful Master! Is it not worth all our labours and sufferings, to come with all those souls we instrumentally begat to Christ: and all that we edified, established, confirmed, and comforted in the way to heaven; and say, Lord, here am I, and the children thou hast given me? To hear one spiritual child say, 'Lord this is the minister by whom I believed.' Another, 'This is he, by whom I was edified, established, and comforted. This is the man that resolved my doubts, quickened my dying affections, reduced my soul, when wandering from the truth!

JOHN FLAVEL

A PASTOR WILL FACE MANY CHALLENGES.

Persistence isn't about gritting your teeth to endure challenges and keep going. Instead, it's a commitment to serve faithfully, while discerning what the challenges are and how to face them. Faithfulness and discernment can be the means of a lifetime of fruitful ministry in one church. For some pastors, however, discernment will be the discipline that helps them determine when it's time to leave a church and can help them do so in a way that honors the Lord.

7 STRATEGIES FOR PERSISTING IN ONE PLACE OF MINISTRY

BRIAN CROFT

TRUST THE WORD.

It is tempting to rely upon modern gimmicks and pragmatism to bring life back into their struggling church. But the answer is the same as it was when Paul instructed Timothy to "Preach the Word" (2 Tim 4:2). If we believe God's Word through his Spirit breathes life into a church, then the most important change comes on the new pastor's first Sunday. But time must be given for the Word to do its work.

SHEPHERD SOULS.

In so many cases, the decline and struggle of local churches can be traced to decades of unfaithful shepherds who cared more about numbers, programs, politics, and personal gain than the biblical call for pastors to shepherd the souls of God's people (1 Pet 5:1-4; Heb 13:17). Many churches needing help have hurting, broken, discouraged sheep who need a shepherd to care for them and nurture them back to health. It is a common and costly error to immediately look outside the church for new life, when there are God's sheep longing for that renewed life already within the church.

LOVE ALL PEOPLE.

As we see the imperatives for pastors in Scripture to "shepherd the flock" (1 Pet 5:2) and to do so "as those who will give an account" (Heb 13:17), it is important to recognize that we don't get to pick who we will answer for in the church. Some in a church are more difficult to love than others, but the key to faithful ministry is not just pouring into the teachable and supportive, but pursuing those hard to love and seeking to win those who are cynical towards your ministry.

PRAY HARD.

The despair and discouragement that often accompany difficult pastoral ministry can create a panicked approach that could lead pastors to act hastily and think they have to solve every problem now. Sometimes the best thing to do to be faithful is to stop and pray and cry out to God for your church and your people. In my experience, rarely has a pastor ready to bail at the two-year mark prayed for his flock as he should.

CELEBRATE OLDER MEMBERS.

If a church has been around for many years, inevitably there are long-term older members who long for their church to return to its former glory. These are typically the ones who have kept the struggling church open for many years, but are also the ones who are commonly resistant to needed change. Because of this, these longtime faithful members can appear to be more of a hindrance for renewed life instead of a benefit. Faithfulness in ministry is loving and accepting these longtime members and finding ways to celebrate them.

BE PATIENT.

The longer a pastor stays at his church, the more he will realize he was shown much grace in the earlier years. Patience might be the most important key to perseverance, as it will cause a pastor to wait when he needs to wait. It will cause a pastor to make decisions with a longer view in mind. Patience will cause a pastor not to give up on a difficult person just yet. Patience is not just a significant fruit of the spirit in every Christian's life, but a key element to both surviving and avoiding great discouragement.

EXPECT SUFFERING.

If you are a pastor trying to persevere in a local church holding on to the hope suffering will not come, you should find another line of work now. In many cases, the reason pastors are ready to resign after about two years of ministry in one place is because they finally meet the adversaries the enemy had placed. As many pastors begin to talk through the discouragement and struggles, we eventually ask them, "Did you think becoming the pastor of that church would not bring adversaries?" Expect suffering in this noble work of pastoral ministry so when it does come, you will not be shocked and preparation for this suffering can lead to your perseverance through it.

PREPARATION FOR
THIS SUFFERING
CAN LEAD TO YOUR
PERSEVERANCE
THROUGH IT.

AUTOPSY OF A BURNED OUT PASTOR

13 LESSONS

THOM RAINER

[THIS ARTICLE WAS ORIGINALLY PUBLISHED AT
THOMRAINER.COM ON JUNE 23, 2014.]

Perhaps the autopsy metaphor is not the best choice. After all, the person is not deceased. But the pastor who is burned out feels like life is draining out. Unfortunately, I have spoken with too many pastors for whom burnout is a reality or a near reality.

What lessons can we learn from those pastors who burned out? Allow me to share 13 lessons I have learned from those who have met this fate. They are in no particular order.

1. The pastor would not say "no" to requests for time. Being a short-term people-pleaser became a longer-term problem.

2. The pastor had no effective way to deal with critics. What types of systems do effective leaders put in place to deal with criticisms so they respond when necessary, but don't deplete their emotional reservoirs?

3. The pastor served a dysfunctional church. Any pastor who leads a church that remains dysfunctional over a long period of time is likely headed toward burnout.

4. The pastor did little or no physical exercise. I understand this dilemma, because I have been there in the recent past.

5 The pastor did not have daily Bible time. I continue to be amazed, but not surprised, how this discipline affects our spiritual health, emotional health, and leadership ability.

6 The pastor's family was neglected. "If anyone does not know how to manage his own household, how will he take care of God's church?" (1 Tim 3:5 HCSB).

7 The pastor rarely took a day off. No break in the routine and demands of pastoring is a path for burnout.

8 The pastor rarely took a vacation. Again, the issues are similar to the failure to take a day off.

9 The pastor never took a sabbatical. After several years of the intense demands of serving a church, a sabbatical of a few weeks is critical to the emotional, spiritual, and physical health of a pastor.

10 The pastor never learned effective relational and leadership skills. When that is the case, conflict and weak vocational performance are inevitable. That, in turn, leads to burnout.

11 The pastor was negative and argumentative. Negativity and an argumentative spirit drain a pastor. That negativity can be expressed in conversations, sermons, blogs, or any communication venue. Argumentative pastors are among the first to experience burnout.

12 The pastor was not a continuous learner. Pastors who fail to learn continuously are not nearly as energized as those who do. Again, this disposition can lead to burnout.

13 The pastor was not paid fairly. Financial stress can lead to burnout quickly.

Many pastors are leaving ministry because they have experienced burnout. Many others are just on the edge of burnout. Pastors need our continuous support and prayers. And they themselves need to avoid the 13 issues noted here.

How are people to observe the outcome of our lives and faith (Heb 13:7) if we don't stay long enough for them to know us? I fear that too many pastors have let market-driven thinking put a premium on new, novel, and innovative, and thus they undervalue faithful, reliable, constant, and certain. No doubt, sometimes it's the right thing to move on. But more often, our penchant to move shows that we're relying on programs more than preaching. We're looking for seed that springs up quickly rather than the slower-growing and hearty fruit of elders and ministers, faithful mothers and fathers, and generations of blessing to a community through a faithful ministry.

MARK DEVER

STAY OR GO

HOW TO (NOT) HANDLE THE DECISION

BY MICHAEL LAWRENCE

COMMON MISTAKES PASTORS MAKE WHEN DECIDING WHETHER TO STAY OR LEAVE A PASTORAL ROLE

1. MAKING A PRIVATE, INDIVIDUAL DECISION. Maybe he talks to his wife, old seminary professors, buddies from seminary, or fellow pastors of other churches, but they will all be people outside the church. He fails to talk to the people that matter the most besides his wife, and that is his own congregation: fellow leadership and the whole congregation.

2. MAKING THE DECISION IN TERMS OF ALL THE NEGATIVES he sees at their current church and all the potential positives at the other church.

3. THINKING PURELY IN TERMS OF "BIGGER EQUALS BETTER." More money, more staff. Some of those things are fine things in and of themselves, but they're not fundamentally how to decide whether to go to another church.

4. BELIEVING ALL THE WONDERFUL THINGS that the search committee is saying to him, and believing everything the critics say at the current church about him. Neither side is telling the whole story.

HOW TO MAKE
THE DECISION

1. This needs to be a matter of sustained prayer.

2. Early on, you need to pull wise counselors into the conversation: your wife, your senior pastor (if you're not the senior pastor), your fellow elders, other key church leaders. Eventually, the congregation as a whole needs to be a part of the decision-making process.

3. You need to be clear on why you want to leave and what constitutes a sufficient reason to leave.

LEGITIMATE
CONSIDERATIONS

1. The door has been closed to ministry.

2. Your gifts are not being given good scope and freedom to be used, and so there's a stewardship issue.

3. You're no longer in accord doctrinally with the church.

4. The church is not able to adequately care for and support your family.

QUESTIONS TO ASK BEFORE DECIDING TO LEAVE

JEFF ROBINSON

1

Do you have any substantive support in the church? Are there godly people in the church who support you and "have your back?" If there are even a few, you might consider staying and asking God for patience.

2

Is this ministry taking a toll on your marriage or chewing up your family? Your marriage will need to be strong in the ministry. Paul makes clear in the list of qualifications in 1 Timothy 3, if the little flock at home is not in order, then you are no longer qualified for ministry. If a difficult season is taking a toll on your marriage or family, it may be time to go.

3

Is there a mitigating factor that could prevent you from staying? One example might be that your church is financially broke and you are unable to find supplementary income. This certainly does not mean you must leave, but it could be God's way of removing you. External, mitigating factors such as this need to be handled carefully, with much thought, discernment, and prayer.

4

Have you sought the counsel of mature, godly pastors? If so, what was their advice? If you are relatively new to the ministry, this is especially important, and you should take their counsel seriously.

5

Has God given you the gifts necessary to help your church or will your continued leadership only harm it further? This is not so much a factor if you have plural leadership, but can be an important question to ponder if you are a single elder. It could be that your leadership style needs to grow in fidelity to the biblical model of patience, humility, and servant-heartedness.

5 REASONS TO PLANT YOUR LIFE IN A CHURCH AND STAY THERE

HERSHAEL W. YORK

NOT EVERY PASTOR HAS THE OPTION TO STAY IN the same church for a long time. God might call you somewhere else, a church filled with unregenerate or unresponsive members might force you to leave, or health needs of family members might dictate a move. I do not mean to lay false guilt on those who have legitimate reasons to leave a church or go elsewhere. I do, however, mean to encourage pastors to default to staying rather than leaving, even in the face of problems. Here's why:

 ONE

The longer you live in community with people, the more credibility you will have. There are no shortcuts to credibility, but every day presents plenty of shortcuts to its loss.

 TWO

You will know for certain what the church has been taught and can intentionally plan your preaching so they learn a strategic grasp of the Scripture and its redemptive-historical framework.

THREE

Nearly every pastor will face a crisis of leadership in the church at a 1-year, 3-year, 5-year, and 9-year mark (give or take a year at each point). If a pastor leaves at the 3-year crisis, then he has to start all over again somewhere else, with crises there. He may be in danger of one day claiming to have 30 years of experience in ministry, when in fact he has 3 years of experience 10 times.

FOUR

The temptation to preach old sermons at a new church setting is too great for some to resist, but rehashing old, familiar stuff will lead to spiritual dryness. Preaching old sermons leaves more discretionary time, but it's time that a pastor doesn't usually want anyone to know he has. Consequently, he'll fall into a pattern of looking busy when he's not, at best wasting time on silly things, at worst spending time on illicit things. Sin usually flows in the direction of discretionary time. The necessity to be fresh and preach books, sections, and texts that the congregation has never heard before is a tremendous grace and discipline in a pastor's life, but that necessity is only there when he stays someplace for a longer period than he has sermons for.

FIVE

Moving is tough on families. I certainly applaud those men who do it out of the necessity of a calling, but I pity the families of men who do it out of personal ambition, laziness, or greed. A pastor's wife, for instance, has enough challenges facing her in developing meaningful friendships and having ministry impact without also having to start over every 3 years.

> The standards you set for yourself and your ministry are directly related to your view of God.
>
> PAUL TRIPP

EXCEL

> Whatever you do, work heartily, as for the Lord and not for men.
>
> COLOSSIANS 3:23

PART THREE

LENCE

Work that is
truly Christian is
work well done.

R. KENT HUGHES

EXCEL STILL MORE

BY

DANIEL S. DUMAS

> The legitimate motive
> for excellence is to seek
> achievement for the end to
> glorify God. One thing that
> does not bear witness to
> the glory of God is a human
> addiction to mediocrity,
> a smug satisfaction
> with the status quo.
>
> **R.C. SPROUL**

WHAT EXCELLENCE DEMANDS

> Make not this man
> or that man your mode;
> be yourself, and aim and
> reach toward the true
> model of all excellence,
> that is, Christ Jesus.
>
> **J.L. LENHART**

There's no doubt "excellence" is a word in vogue. Pick up a book on leadership, productivity, or most things, really, and you'll run into that word frequently. It's officially a buzzword.

What, then, is this word doing in a book about pastoral ministry?

When I use the word "excellence," I mean doing the right thing, the right way, at the right time. When I think about striving for excellence in ministry, I don't have in mind some worldly standard to which gospel ministry must bow, but a benevolent ambition for the glory of God in all things.

What I have in mind is "Whatever you do, work heartily, as for the Lord and not for men," (Col 3:23) and, "Whatever you do, in word or deed, do everything in the name of the Lord Jesus" (Col 3:17), and "So, whether you eat or drink, or whatever you do, do all to the glory of God" (1 Cor 10:31). In those verses is a call to excellence. It's a call for gospel ministers to work in a way worthy of the one they serve.

This kind of biblical excellence is not something you strive for only when you've got high-profile events and occasions that need to look good; it's a matter of DNA. It's a philosophy of ministry. Excellence must permeate and animate all of your service and leadership in the church. It should be a constant refrain in your life. This was the case in my house growing up, with my dad often telling us, "If something is worth doing, it's worth doing it right." If you value excellence and the glory of God, your actions will follow.

How would you define excellence? Is this something you prioritize in your life and ministry?

_____

_____

_____

_____

_____

_____

_____

_____

_____

_____

_____

_____

_____

_____

_____

_____

_____

_____

_____

_____

_____

_____

> If a man is willing to pay the price of fatigue and weariness, his ministry will not be mediocre.
>
> **JOHN MACARTHUR**

The pursuit of excellence requires investment. It's not something that happens overnight, but is a total shift in perspective and commitment. It's your responsibility as a spiritual leader to set the cultural tone of excellence.

What does excellence demand?

First, it demands a meticulous attention to detail. You cannot be sloppy and be excellent. There's something to be said for the fact that the God went to such great lengths to describe the way Moses was to build the tabernacle. A hefty portion of Exodus 25-40 is the Lord's instructions for the design and construction of the tabernacle. Don't think God doesn't care about details. Your attention to detail can't be overbearing and micromanaging, but it also can't be lazy and apathetic. Excellence is not just a macro reality; it starts at the micro level. There's value in doing small things well.

Second, it demands energy and time. You've got to be willing to dig in. J. Oswald Sanders says that if a man "is unwilling to pay the price of fatigue for his leadership, it will always be mediocre." It takes time and energy to do things right. Haste is a great enemy of excellence. There are no shortcuts to excellence. The appeal to get something done and move on is awfully strong, but there will be a price to pay in the long run. Closely related to the time and energy that excellence demands is thoughtfulness and care. Thinking takes time, but it is always worth the investment. You must acquire discipline to think and to care about the standard you set for yourself and others, and you need a disposition never to settle for mediocrity in ministry.

I saw this modeled in the preaching of John MacArthur. The time and energy he put into his preparation meant that the product was excellent. The pursuit of excellence in his preparation meant that even his "subpar" sermons were better than the good sermons of most other guys. Every time he approaches the Scripture, he does so with care, not twisting it, adding to it, or changing it. He approaches sermon preparation as a craftsman. You can discern the thoughtfulness and quality in the product.

Have you ever bought a shirt for a really good deal? It feels great because you saved a few bucks. But then you wash it and the collar comes out all messed up, one sleeve is longer than the other, and there's a thread coming loose. The thing was cheap because it was cheaply made. If you've ever had a really nice shirt, you know that it's usually worth every penny. They last a long time and the quality doesn't wane. It takes a little more investment up front, but the value increases over time.

So it is with excellence. It takes more energy, time, and attention to detail, but the value will be clear over time, because excellence lasts.

What areas of your life and ministry would benefit from more time, energy, and attention to detail? Does your preaching and teaching need more preparation? Are there ways you could further equip yourself?

Keep a close watch on yourself and on the teaching. Persist in this, for by so doing you will save both yourself and your hearers.

1 TIMOTHY 4:16

> The lazy Christian has his mouth full of complaints, when the active Christian has his heart full of comforts.
>
> **THOMAS BROOKS** 〞

EXCELLENCE SAYS "NO"

> I cannot imagine the Spirit waiting at the door of a sluggard, and supplying the deficiencies of an idle man. Sloth in the cause of the Redeemer is a vice for which no excuse can be invented.
>
> CHARLES H. SPURGEON

Pursuing excellence also means you've got to reject some things. These are things that will undermine any attempt to do all things in the name of Christ.

1. HASTE: Don't be afraid to take time to do something well. Quality over quantity.

2. LAZINESS: Laziness and excellence are mutually exclusive. If you're not sure God cares about laziness and hard work, read Proverbs.

3. BAD THEOLOGY: God cares about excellence; so make room for excellence in your view of God. Look around you. He could have created the world in black and white, but look at the incredible colors he worked into the fabric of creation. He went above and beyond, showing incredible care and thoughtfulness in the things he made.

4. COMPLACENCY: Develop a healthy dissatisfaction with where things are. In your sanctification keep pursuing areas where you need to grow. In your church, keep addressing things that need to improve. Evaluate your sermons to get better. In your ministry, attack your weaknesses and seek opportunities to sharpen yourself.

Do any of these weaknesses ring true for you? Where does it come out in your life and ministry?

For this I toil, struggling with all his energy that he powerfully works within me.

COLOSSIANS 1:29

THROUGHOUT CREATION
GOD WENT ABOVE AND
BEYOND, SHOWING
INCREDIBLE CARE AND
THOUGHTFULNESS IN
THE THINGS HE MADE.

EXCELLENCE AND YOUR PEOPLE

> But by the grace of God I am what I am, and his grace toward me was not in vain. On the contrary, I worked harder than any of them, though it was not I, but the grace of God that is with me.
>
> **1 CORINTHIANS 15:10**

Excellence in the ministry is others-oriented. It's not just about caring for yourself, but about the lives and experience of your people. You want your people to feel welcome and cared-for, and that their pastors are working hard, not doing just enough to get by. A pastor who's sloppy in his sermon preparation and delivery will cause his hearers to wonder what other areas he's compromising.

Your people know excellence when they see it. They might not be able to articulate exactly what makes something excellent, but they can recognize it. Maybe your facilities need to improve. In order to have a nice bathroom, you don't need $8,000 toilets. But you can clean the place, make sure it's got supplies, make sure it smells good, put some colors on the wall, add a few amenities to the counter, and your people will know you care about their experience at the church.

There are, of course, things more important than your bathrooms. You serve people who will spend eternity somewhere, and you are a significant influence in how they prepare for it. For that reason, it's good to not only pursue excellence in your own life and ministry, but to create a culture of excellence.

How do you do this?

CULTURE OF EXCELLENCE

1. Search the Scripture and be convinced of the importance of excellence yourself.

2. Teach it to your people. It's not a one-sermon job, it's constant education.

3. Set a higher standard. Don't simply meet the lowest common denominator; try to raise it. Give your people an appetite for excellence (good preaching, good music, thoughtful leadership).

4. Be an example. Don't demand or ask for something you're not willing to do. If you want your people to read the Bible better, show them from the pulpit how you read and study the Bible.

5. Keep teaching the Scripture. Over and over.

6. Be patient. It takes time to get where you want to go. The Lord is patient with you, so extend the same.

7. Be gracious. Pursue excellence, not perfectionism.

Regardless of where your allegiance lies in college football, you've got to respect the University of Alabama. They know how to win. One writer described the Alabama football program as a place "where excellence is a starting point rather than a superlative."

That should be your goal in your life and in your ministry. Mediocrity should be a total aberration; your people should expect excellence, not because they want you to meet some worldly standard, but because the Scripture calls you to do all things in the name of the Lord Jesus, to the glory of God.

Whether it is children's or youths' ministries, men's or women's ministries, small groups or outreach, whether it is leadership training or short-term missions, public worship or preaching, I will want each ministry of the church to be done in excellence so that they will faithfully display the excellence of the One who calls out of darkness into his marvelous light.

PAUL TRIPP

WHERE
EXCELLENCE IS A
STARTING POINT
RATHER THAN A
SUPERLATIVE

UNDERSTANDING EXCELLENCE

JAMES M. HAMILTON JR.

One who says that their commitment to the primacy of preaching leads them to have little regard for the music, parking, greeting, signage, aesthetics, friendliness, hands-on ministry, evangelism, outreach, care-giving, announcements, and so on, is simply theologizing their laziness and apathy.

DAVID PRINCE

EXCELLENCE DEFINED

The word "excellence" makes me nervous because worldly standards can so easily become the blood pumping through our hearts. Discussing excellence can also portray arrogance, as though the one talking about excellence thinks he's excellent and everyone else needs to come up to his standard.

But if Christ is our standard, and if we can remember that God looks on the heart and chooses what is weak in the eyes of the world, perhaps we can ask ourselves this question:

Can you imagine Jesus doing anything of inferior quality?

As a carpenter or a public speaker, as a student of the Scripture or one in communion with his Father in prayer, as a family member or a friend, in every way Jesus set the standard for how we measure excellence. Christ has defined excellence, and we seek to be conformed to his image. Excellence as we measure it, then, is Christlikeness.

EXAMPLES OF EXCELLENCE

In addition to Jesus, we can follow hard-working Paul as he followed Christ. Blameless Joseph is a type of the one in whose footsteps we walk. Moses was trained in all the wisdom of Egypt and put his learning to work in the writing of the Pentateuch. Nehemiah applied his administrative chops to build the wall. Ezra set his heart to know, do, and teach. The depth of John's pondering invites us to marinate in God's love. On and on we could go like this. ... Excellence is everywhere in the Scripture inspired by the God who is himself excellent.

DANGERS OF PURSUING EXCELLENCE

For those who follow the one who was crucified, we cannot measure excellence by the world's approval, values, or attainments. Excellence has to be defined by the Bible's story and demands rather than the world. Death is gain. The poor in spirit are blessed. Trials are occasions for joy. Suffering produces character and hope. The way up is the way down because the rich became poor so that the poor could be rich.

This means that excellence is not necessarily what would impress the folks at ESPN, the political operatives in D.C., or the culture-makers in NYC. Excellence is that elusive pursuit of the way of life that results in the one whose opinion matters saying: Well done, good and faithful servant.

CONSISTENT EXCELLENCE

Here we have to be guided by the qualifications for ministry in 1 Timothy 3 and Titus 1. This means that the pursuit of excellence in some areas can never eclipse pursuit of it in all others: An obsession with excellence in preaching, for instance, could result in a neglect of people, even a rudeness, that results in a man not being above reproach. Similarly, a desire to be excellent at caring for the needs of the flock could be pursued at the expense of paying excellent attention to your wife — listening to her — or doing an excellent job as a father to your children. So we should ask ourselves whether we are pursuing excellence at every point: marriage, parenting, self-control, hospitality, teaching, dealing with others, stewardship, and our dealings with outsiders.

God help us. And praise be to him for his grace.

THE BY-PRODUCT
OF A HIGH VIEW
OF GOD IS A
CONSTANT AND
RELENTLESS PURSUIT
OF EXCELLENCE
IN ALL THINGS.

RECOMMENDED RESOURCES

Brothers, We Are Not Professionals, John Piper

Church Planter: The Man, the Message, the Mission, Darrin Patrick

The Conviction to Lead: 25 Principles for Leadership that Matters,
R. Albert Mohler Jr.

The Cross and Christian Ministry, D.A. Carson

*Dangerous Calling: Confronting the Unique Challenges
of Pastoral Ministry*, Paul David Tripp

A Guide to Expository Ministry, Daniel S. Dumas, ed.

He Is Not Silent: Preaching in a Postmodern World, R. Albert Mohler Jr.

Lectures to My Students, C.H. Spurgeon

The Missionary Call: Find Your Place in God's Plan for the World,
M. David Sills

Nine Marks of a Healthy Church, Mark Dever

Preaching and Preachers, D. Martyn Lloyd-Jones

Preaching: How to Preach Biblically, John MacArthur

Shepherds After My Own Heart, Timothy Laniak

CONTRIBUTORS

R. ALBERT MOHLER JR. is the ninth president of The Southern Baptist Theological Seminary, where he also serves as a professor of Christian theology. Mohler is the author of *We Cannot Be Silent*, *Conviction to Lead: 25 Principles for Leadership that Matters*, *He is Not Silent*, *Culture Shift*, and *Desire and Deceit*. Mohler hosts two podcasts: "The Briefing," and "Thinking in Public." He also writes a popular blog with regular commentary on moral, cultural, and theological issues at www.AlbertMohler.com. Mohler is an ordained minister, and has served as pastor and staff minister of several Southern Baptist churches. He is married to Mary and has two children and one grandson.

🐦 @ALBERTMOHLER

HERSHAEL W. YORK is the Victor and Louise Lester Professor of Christian Preaching at The Southern Baptist Theological Seminary and senior pastor of Buck Run Baptist Church in Frankfort, Kentucky. Before coming to Southern, he served as president of the Kentucky Baptist Convention and pastor of Ashland Avenue Baptist Church in Lexington, Kentucky. He and his wife, Tanya, have raised two sons.

🐦 @HERSHAELYORK

DANIEL S. DUMAS is senior vice president for Institutional Administration and professor of Christian ministry and leadership. He also serves as a teaching pastor and elder at Crossing Church in Louisville, Kentucky. He is the author of *Live Smart* and co-author of *A Guide to Biblical Manhood* and editor of *A Guide to Expository Ministry*. He came to Louisville from Grace Community Church in Sun Valley, California, where he served as elder, executive pastor, pastor of assimilation, director of conferences and pastor of the Cornerstone Fellowship Group. He is married to Jane and has two children.

🐦 @DANDUMAS

PRODUCTION

PROJECT EDITOR

MATT DAMICO is associate pastor of worship at Kenwood Baptist Church in Louisville.. He earned a Bachelor of Arts in English from the University of Minnesota in 2008 before moving to Louisville. He graduated from Southern with a Master of Divinity in 2012. He is married to Anna and they have two daughters.

DESIGNER

LAURA JOHNS is a graphic designer at The Village Church in Flower Mound, Texas. A Nebraska native, Johns earned her Bachelor of Science in Graphic Design from John Brown University. She is married to Bryan, and they are the proud parents of Cole Alexander.